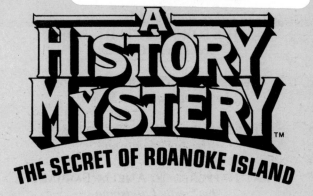

A HISTORY MYSTERY™

THE SECRET OF ROANOKE ISLAND

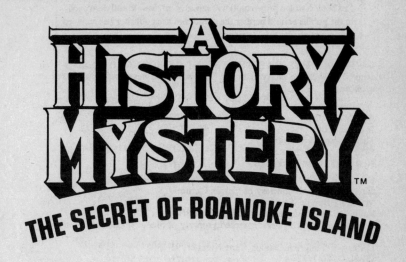

A HISTORY MYSTERY™

THE SECRET OF ROANOKE ISLAND

JANET HUBBARD-BROWN

AN AVON CAMELOT BOOK

A HISTORY MYSTERY: THE SECRET OF ROANOKE ISLAND is an
original publication of Avon Books. This work has never before appeared in
book form.

AVON BOOKS
A division of
The Hearst Corporation
1350 Avenue of the Americas
New York, New York 10019

Copyright © 1991 by Whitbread Books/Shannon Gilligan
Cover photograph courtesy of Culver Pictures
Mazes by Bonnie Atwater
Published by arrangement with Whitbread Books
A History Mystery is a trademarked property of Shannon Gilligan/Whitbread
Books
Library of Congress Catalog Card Number: 91-7892
ISBN: 0-380-76223-4
RL: 5.7

Library of Congress Cataloging in Publication Data:

Hubbard-Brown, Janet.
    The secret of Roanoke Island / Janet Hubbard-Brown.
        p.   cm.—(A History mystery) (An Avon Camelot book)
    Includes bibliographical references.
    Summary: Describes the events surrounding the mysterious disappearance
of the small group of English colonists who settled on Roanoke Island in
1587.
    1. Roanoke Colony (N.C.)—Juvenile literature. [1. Roanoke Colony
(N.C.)]
I. Title.   II. Series.
F229.H84 1991
975.6′175—dc20   91-7892
                                                                          CIP
                                                                           AC

First Avon Camelot Printing: November 1991

CAMELOT TRADEMARK REG. U.S. PAT. OFF. AND IN OTHER COUNTRIES,
MARCA REGISTRADA, HECHO EN U.S.A.

Printed in the U.S.A.

OPM   10   9   8   7   6   5   4   3   2   1

I would like to acknowledge most gratefully the help of the following: Harriet Hubbard Matthews of Chapel Hill, N.C., for introducing me to the Outer Banks; librarians, Manteo Public Library, for their cheerful assistance; Shannon Gilligan of Whitbread Books for her editing skill; Valerie Andrews for her warm support, Betsy Tonn, librarian, Joslin Memorial Library, Waitsfield, Vermont, for her friendly efficiency; my friends at Concepts Publishing—Jill Bobrow, Dana Jinkins and Cheryl Rousseau—for their generosity; and last but never least, my family—Frank, Luke and Ramsey for their adaptability and support.

Table of Contents

The manner of their attire and painting them selues when they goe to their generall huntings, or at theire Solemne feasts.

A painting by John White of the typical dress of a native of the Roanoke Island region.

Chronology

1492—Christopher Columbus, financed by the King and Queen of Spain, lands in the Bahama Islands, off the coast of current-day Florida. He discovers Haiti and Cuba on the same trip.

1524—Gerolamo de Verrazzano, a Spaniard, sees the shores of the Outer Banks of North Carolina for the first time.

1566—Fernandes, a Portuguese pilot who later had a crucial impact on the settlers at Roanoke, first learns of the Outer Banks from a Spanish pilot.

1580—Fernandes is sent by Sir Walter Raleigh of England to look for a suitable location for a new colony.

1584—Arthur Barlowe and Philip Amadas, two Englishmen also working for Raleigh, land on Roanoke Island and stay three months. When they return to England, they bring two Native Americans, Manteo and Wanchese.

1585-1586—Sir Richard Grenville and Ralph Lane set up an English colony on Roanoke Island. Trouble with the native inhabitants brews. They are finally rescued by Sir Francis Drake.

1587—John White, an English artist, returns to Roanoke as governor to establish yet a third colony. He comes with 114 settlers, including his daughter, Eleanor White Dare.

1587—July 23rd, George Howe, one of the new settlers, is killed while crabbing.

CHRONOLOGY

1587—August 14th, Virginia Dare, Eleanor's daughter, is the first English child born in the New World.

1587—Late August, John White is forced to return to England for supplies.

1588—White attempts to return to Roanoke, and is turned back by a terrible storm.

1588—The Spanish attack England and are defeated.

1590—White finally manages to return to Roanoke Island. He finds "Croatoan" carved in a tree, but no sign of any colonists, including his daughter.

1602—Sir Walter Raleigh's final attempt to check on the Roanoke settlers is thwarted by another terrible storm on the Outer Banks.

1607—Jamestown is founded (near modern Williamsburg) and becomes the first permanent colony in the new land.

1890—Interest in the disappearance at Roanoke is rekindled after several hundred years by one historian's contention that descendants of the Roanoke colonists are living in Robeson County, North Carolina.

1937—Paul Green writes "The Lost Colony," a play depicting the plight of the Roanoke settlers.

1938—A man claims to find a stone on the banks of a Virginia river with an inscription written by John White's daughter, Eleanor. Forty-nine stones are found in all, but historians later discredit the find as a hoax.

1941—The Roanoke settlement becomes an official National Historic Site to commemorate Sir Walter Raleigh's colonies in the New World and as the birthplace of Virginia Dare, the first English citizen born on American shores.

1990—The fascination with the lost colony at Roanoke is as strong as ever.

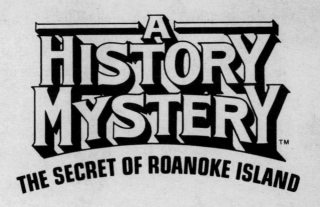

A HISTORY MYSTERY™

THE SECRET OF ROANOKE ISLAND

Stranded!

For three years, Governor John White had only one thing on his mind. He had to return to Virginia. Over one hundred people were waiting for him there. He was supposed to come with supplies and more people from England. His beloved daughter Eleanor was waiting for him. So was his new granddaughter Virginia Dare. Virginia had been born soon after the settlers had arrived on Roanoke Island. She was the first English child born in the New World. That was something to brag about! Virginia would be three years old now and running all over the place. She might even have a new brother or sister.

John White and his group of settlers had arrived on the southeastern shore of North America in July 1587. They hadn't been there long before the settlers realized that they would need more supplies. The settlers decided that someone would have to return to England for supplies. That someone was their governor, John White.

White looked impatiently out the window of his London house. He was waiting for the arrival of Sir Walter Raleigh. If Sir Walter wouldn't help him this time, White would have to give up the idea of returning to his family and friends forever. He wished for the thousandth time that he had followed his instincts and refused to leave Virginia. Someone else should have come. Why did he allow the other settlers to talk him into being the one to return? Who could know that he would end up stuck back in England? Were the Assistants he left behind doing a good job? He wondered if the colonists had moved up to the Chesapeake Bay area by now. They had talked about it many times. Roanoke Island wasn't a good place for a colony. They knew that from the beginning.

If their wretched pilot, Fernandes, hadn't played a trick on John White, they wouldn't have settled there at all. White had complained to everyone he could think of about Fernandes dropping them at Roanoke Island instead of the Chesapeake area. Fernandes just dumped the settlers there and sailed on.

White had been wounded three times during his last attempt to bring supplies to the Roanoke settlers. That had only been a year ago, in 1589. In fact, every effort over the past three years to return to his family and friends had been foiled. What made it most frustrating was that every time he came close to leaving, something would happen at the last minute to prevent it.

Things had gone wrong from the start. Right after White had arrived back in England in November 1587, Queen Elizabeth announced that no vessels could leave English ports. England and Spain were about to go to war. Elizabeth wanted her nation's ships and soldiers close to home in case of an attack.

Sir Walter Raleigh, who owned the patent to the land of Virginia, stepped in. He had a strong influence on Queen Elizabeth. He knew about the Chesapeake Bay area. Sir Walter Raleigh also thought it would make a good military base. Spain was a big threat abroad as well as in England. The Spaniards could be in Virginia now for all the English knew. Communication between England and the New World was very slow, if it happened at all. The English knew there was already a Spanish colony north of Florida. So far, they hadn't been able to find it. They could only guess about what was happening in America.

Raleigh arranged for White to leave right away with supplies for the colonists. Other, larger ships would follow as part of the plan for establishing a military base. White had arranged for a new group of English citizens to take the voyage.

THE SECRET OF ROANOKE ISLAND

By late March 1588, everything seemed ready. But at the last moment, the plan went awry. The voyage was canceled. It would be dangerous sailing no matter what, for the seas were a war zone. Privateering, or raiding other ships, was big business. *Privateer* was the name for those pilots who overtook and robbed other ships. Before Queen Elizabeth made such actions legal, these same men were called pirates.

What probably really delayed White's voyage was high wind. And before the winds had calmed, orders came from the queen for them to stop their plans to leave.

White was horribly upset. What about the colonists? Had they survived the winter? Four months had passed since he had arrived back in England. The voyage home had been filled with disasters. It had taken much longer than planned. The colonists had expected him back long ago.

White didn't give up. He contacted everyone until, finally, two small ships were made available to him. They were called the *Roe* and the *Brave*. Most of the persons who had planned to sail on the bigger ships dropped out this time. Only seven men and four women decided to sail. They were probably relatives or close friends of the settlers who had left the year before.

The *Roe* and the *Brave* left England on April 22, 1589. It had taken White a whole year to get the trip

Sir Walter Raleigh, the Englishman who owned the lease on the island of Roanoke, along with much of the surrounding area. Raleigh lost interest in settling the region, and turned his attention to Ireland and South America instead.

organized. He carried letters from Sir Walter Raleigh to the settlers in the colony, informing them that more supplies were on their way.

Unfortunately, once they were on their way, the two ships' captains turned out to be more interested in robbery than in the colonists they were going to help. Instead of sailing for America, the *Roe* and the *Brave* chased every vessel in sight. Every ship the two captains came upon, they boarded and robbed. Then they attacked a French ship. A bloody battle followed, and White was badly wounded. The English had to surrender. Everything was taken from them, including all the supplies meant for the colonists. With their crippled ship, they set sail for England. On May 22, they arrived back on the English coast. It was a miracle that they had made it at all.

Because the Spanish Armada had attacked England the year before, Raleigh and everyone else were concentrating on fighting the Spanish. White's disastrous voyage did not create the attention it would have in peacetime. Queen Elizabeth still did not want ships leaving England. That was why White was meeting with Raleigh one more time. Perhaps Raleigh knew of a way for White to sail again.

White's passion to return to the colony was intense. Raleigh knew what White wanted—to take more supplies and more people to Virginia. Raleigh knew White had family there.

Raleigh put White in touch with a man named

William Sanderson. Sanderson was part of a privateering syndicate, and could be made willing to
help—for a price.

It took a great deal of money to send a fleet of ships
across the ocean. White made a good living as an
artist, but he didn't have that kind of money. After
their meeting, Raleigh helped organize a group of
men who would contribute money to the crossing. In
return, they would be able to trade freely with the
city of Raleigh and other parts of Virginia.

In truth, Raleigh didn't help more because he had
developed new interests. He was more interested in
Ireland and South America than he was in a hundred people stranded in Virginia. He wanted to keep
his patent on that land. But the patent was good
until 1603.

White hated the politics surrounding these human
lives. Something always seemed more important.

Raleigh talked to William Sanderson on behalf of
White. Sanderson agreed to help and found White a
ship. White renamed the ship the *Moonlight* and
began to equip her. It wasn't easy to find the necessary guns and equipment with England at war.

White also needed a captain. He was pleased to get
a man named Edward Spicer for the job. Spicer had
sailed back from Roanoke Island in 1587 with White.
They were good friends.

Still, another ship was needed. Sir Walter asked
his friend John Watts, another privateer, to help.

Watts offered his ship, called the *Hopewell*. Abraham Cocke was her captain. She was to carry artillery to be used to set up a post on the Chesapeake Bay. Around eighty men were on board. Two other ships carrying arms and men were to accompany them.

The plan was for the fleet of four ships to do their privateering work. At the same time, the ships would slowly make their way to Roanoke Island to check on the settlers.

It was the end of February 1590. At last, after more than two years, White would be seeing his family and friends. The past two years had been the most difficult of his life. But now he could put that behind him. Perhaps he had been the right man to send back to England after all. Who else could have stood all the frustration? It had taken great patience and effort to come this far.

He arrived at the dock with the new settlers for the colony. They had their equipment and belongings with them. Abraham Cocke was waiting.

The group was in for a shock. Captain Cocke informed White that the new colonists could not go. Cocke claimed privateering was too dangerous. John White was ready to argue with the captain. Both Sir Walter Raleigh and William Sanderson had given their permission for the voyage to begin.

But Captain Cocke's mind was made up. He would not carry the colonists to Virginia. White was crestfallen. So were his followers.

STRANDED!

White wondered why everything had to be such a fight. He had not wanted to leave the colony in the first place. But he had allowed himself to be talked into it. He hadn't wanted the colonists to settle on Roanoke Island either. But a Spanish pilot tricked him, forcing them to settle there. Now another bloke was telling him he couldn't bring his friends aboard when it had already been approved.

It was too late to contact Raleigh or Watts to see if either could convince Cocke to change his mind. White couldn't bear the thought of missing another departure after so many years of trying to return to America. He would have to obey the captain. "I'm sorry," he told the other settlers. "Captain's orders." He turned and boarded the ship.

The *Hopewell,* carrying White, sailed first. It wasn't long before the *Moonlight* caught up with her. The ships overtook many Spanish vessels during the voyage. The captains and crew were pleased with their prizes. Finally, in late July 1590, Cocke headed toward Florida.

Once again, White's timing was off. It was hurricane season. The ships couldn't get close to shore. Finally, on August 12, the ships began to navigate the dangerous shoals that branch out from Cape Hatteras. They sailed on until the ships were opposite the inlet at the northern end of Croatoan. Croatoan was the island home of Manteo, a native who had been a good friend to the English. In fact, there had been talk of the settlers moving to Croatoan in

A map of the Atlantic Ocean showing both Great Britain and Roanoke Island. During the late sixteenth century, ships would travel down along the coast of France and Spain, and on to the Canary and Cape Verde Islands.

Iceland

Faeroe Is.

Shetland Is.
Orkney Is.

Great
Britain

Ireland

Sweden

Norway

EUROPE

France

Genoa

Spain

Mediterranean
Sea

Flores   Azores

E
TH
TIC

Canary Is.

AFRICA

Cape Verde Is.

From there, they would cross to one of the Carribbean
islands like Jamaica or Cuba, and finally head north along
the coast of Florida until they reached unsettled territory.

case of trouble. Was there any chance they were there? White looked for any sign of life. But he saw nothing.

Three days later, the ships anchored off Hatarask. Hatarask used to be called Port Ferdinando. But White couldn't stand anything named after Fernandes. He changed the name in his journals to Hatarask, and refused to call it anything else. From Hatarask they could see columns of smoke in the direction of Roanoke Island. White was thrilled.

White, Captain Spicer, and Captain Cocke set out the next morning in smaller boats. They went up Roanoke Sound to see if they could spot the settlers. Smoke was rising in the distance. The group landed and marched toward the smoke. They found nothing except burning brushwood. It could have been caused by lightning. They couldn't even find fresh water. They returned exhausted.

Then Fate stepped in again, changing everything. A fierce wind blew in from the northeast, overturning the *Moonlight.* Some of the men tried to swim ashore and were drowned. Captain Spicer and the steersman hung onto the boat. It rolled over and over and soon they were lost. Seven out of the eleven men aboard the *Moonlight,* including Spicer, drowned.

The rest of the crew did not want to go on. White was desperate. He had lost his loyal friend Spicer and most of his crew. He wasn't so sure of Cocke's men. If they gave up now, all would be lost. But

STRANDED!

Cocke helped convince his crew to stay a little longer. Nineteen men climbed aboard another small boat and made their way up Roanoke Sound.

The group could see a large fire inland. They thought it had to be the colonists. They began to celebrate. They blew their trumpets. All through the night they sang favorite English songs. They called out to the colonists over and over. The next morning they went ashore as soon as the sun rose. The men could see grass and trees burning. White walked on, his heart full of determination.

Suddenly, he stopped. On the beach he saw tracks. He thought they were Indian tracks. And they were fresh.

White hurried on. Up ahead was a dune covered with trees. White stopped. He looked at the faces around him. The three years of frustration seemed to melt away in a few seconds. Filled with anticipation, he began to run to the clearing straight ahead that he had briefly called home three years before.

"Eleanor!" he called. "Eleanor!" He reached the top of the dune and looked down on the settlement. No one was there.

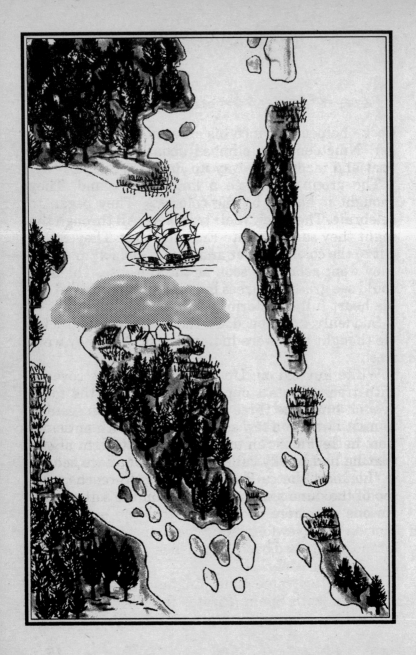

New Settlement
in a New World

The new land of Virginia ran from Spanish Florida north to the New England coast and as far west as the Pacific Ocean. Sir Walter Raleigh began making plans in 1584 to send a few small ships over to the New World. Their assignment was to find a good place for a permanent settlement. Ships from various countries had cruised the waters between Florida and Newfoundland for many years. But so far, no colony had been established on the southeastern shore of America.

During this same time, England was edging toward war with Spain. Pirates from both countries roamed the seas seeking prizes. Spain had already

A map depicting the arrival of the English in Virginia. The engraving is based on a painting by John White. Roanoke is the larger island to the left, just past the narrow barrier islands.

claimed the land called Florida. Because of Spain's claim, Raleigh and his associates wanted to establish an English base in the New World from which they could attack the Spanish ships.

The problem was navigation. Maps were not very accurate in those days. Spain was the leader in exploring the New World and discovering new sailing routes. Spanish pilots were considered the best in the world. The usual route to America was to head to the Caribbean first, then sail north along the Gulf Stream. The Gulf Stream is an ocean current along the Atlantic coast that makes ships go faster. The same route is often used by ships today.

People like Raleigh had to depend on experienced boat pilots to fill in the missing areas on their maps. Simon Fernandes was trained as a ship's pilot in Portugal. Then he shifted his services to Spain. Fernandes had learned a great deal about navigation in the West Indies from the Spanish. He learned about Carolina's Outer Banks from a Spanish pilot who had landed in that area in 1566. Sometime between 1561 and 1573, Fernandes discovered an Outer Banks inlet. He named it Port Ferdinando.

Fernandes was a pirate with a bad reputation. In 1577, he was brought before an English high court for avoiding customs. The Portuguese ambassador to England said that he had enough information about the pilot to hang him. The ambassador told how Fernandes had once killed seven Portuguese sailors

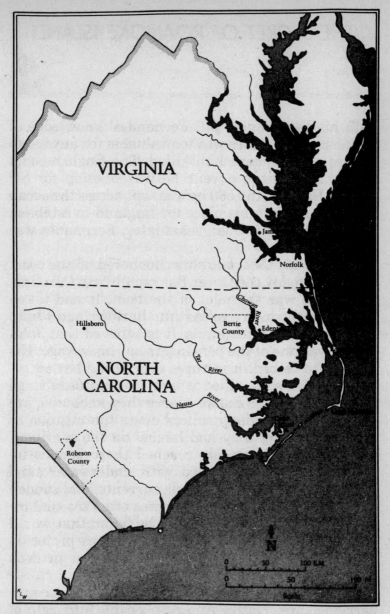

A modern map of the area around Roanoke. Compare it to John White's drawing in the previous picture by turning this map on its side. White was remarkably accurate, considering the crude mapmaking abilities of the day.

with his bare hands. But Fernandes' knowledge of Spanish trade routes was too valuable for anyone to lock him up or have him killed. The English court freed him. Within a year he was piloting for Sir Walter Raleigh. In 1580 he was sent across the ocean to look for a suitable place for England to establish a military colony. Four years later, Fernandes was successful.

On July 13, 1584, two ships anchored off the coast of what is today the Outer Banks of North Carolina. Fernandes was the pilot of the fleet. It had taken three months to arrive. Arthur Barlowe and Philip Amadas were the captains. It is believed that John White was one of the passengers on this voyage. His job was to record in pictures everything he saw.

A smaller ship called a pinnace was used to go inland. The Outer Banks, where they anchored, are barrier islands. Many sailors made the mistake at first of thinking they had landed on the continent when they had actually reached these islands instead. The area was filled with underwater sand bars, spits, rocks, treacherous currents, and sudden unfavorable winds. The water was often too shallow for ships to pass. Inlets had to be found that would allow the larger ships to pass into the more protected sounds. The large ships stayed anchored in deep water in the meantime.

After three days of searching in pinnaces, a canoe carrying three Native Americans came into sight of

Native Americans smoking fish. Smoking was a way to both cook and preserve the day's catch. Based on a drawing by John White.

the large ship and beached. One of the men got out and walked along the shore until he was just opposite. Barlowe, Amadas, Fernandes, and others rowed ashore. The Native Americans showed no fear. They began to speak as the Englishmen approached. They couldn't understand each other, of course. But the Englishmen used sign language to invite them aboard their ship. One of the Native Americans went. They gave him a shirt, a hat, and some wine and returned him to shore. He and the other Native Americans began fishing. They brought a boatload of fish to the Englishmen. The trading had begun. Perhaps friendships would develop. That day was a good start.

THE SECRET OF ROANOKE ISLAND

The following morning, a man named Grandganimeo came. He was the brother of the local chief, Wingina. A few days later, the English returned the courtesy. They left their anchored ships and paid a visit to Wingina's village. They received a wonderful welcome. The English were impressed at the great respect the Native Americans showed for their leaders. Barlowe later wrote, "No people in the world carry more respect to their King, Nobility and Governors, than these do."

When the Englishmen asked the name of the country they were in, one of the Native Americans replied, "Wingandacon." Of course, he didn't understand what he was being asked. His answer, *Wingandacon,* meant, "You wear good clothes." But until Raleigh renamed the land Virginia, it was called Wingandacon by the English.

We now know that around Wingina's time there were about 35,000 Native Americans organized into thirty tribes in this region. They were Algonquians. They all spoke languages that came from a similar basic source. They lived a settled life in villages of one hundred to two hundred people. Agriculture was their main food source. They grew corn, beans, pumpkins, and sunflowers. During the winter, they hunted and went inland to gather roots and nuts. In late winter and early spring, they fished.

White's pictures show the Native Americans with tall, strong, dignified figures. Barlowe described

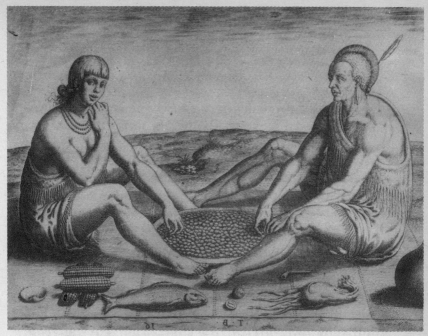

Two Native Americans sharing a meal. Some typical foods set out in front of them include fish, corn, pecans, and even tobacco. From a drawing by John White.

them as "very handsome, and goodly people, and in their behavior as mannerly and civil as any of Europe."

The Native American societies were moving in the direction of statehood in 1584. Rather than continuing with many small tribes, they would become one large community. The chiefs were called werowances. Each werowance governed between six and eight villages.

The Native Americans had had brief contact with Europeans. They had a few tools that they had gotten from a shipwreck years ago. Some Native Americans recalled six years before when three sailors from a shipwreck had come ashore. They stayed three weeks. Then they lashed two canoes together and tried to sail home. They were never seen again.

The English were there for about two months, from early July till late August. It was a perfect time of year. They even managed to do some important exploring. One of the largest settlements the English found was Secotan. John White made many drawings of the village. He and a scientist and mathematician, Thomas Hariot, got to know the natives well. White and Wingina also became close friends. The English met Manteo during this period. He was from a neighboring tribe on Croaton Island. Manteo would remain loyal to the English throughout their efforts to settle there. Perhaps most important of all, Barlowe and Amadas discovered the inlet to the Chesapeake Bay and made friends with the Chesapeake people.

When the time came to return to England, Barlowe and Amadas wanted to bring a couple of the Americans from Wingandacon with them. They took Manteo and a man named Wanchese from Wingina's tribe. Did the two Americans agree to go, or did the English use force? No one knows for sure. It is known that they stayed with Sir Walter Raleigh when they got to England. Hariot studied their language and taught them English. He made a phonetic alphabet of Algonquian so that others could learn to communicate with the natives of America.

Sir Walter Raleigh and other high government officials were pleased with Barlowe's report. Chesapeake Bay looked like a good location for a colony. Raleigh began to assemble a larger expedition to the New World. This time he sent 600 soldiers under the leadership of Sir Richard Grenville. Simon Fernandes was the chief pilot aboard the flagship, the *Tiger*. Also aboard the *Tiger* was Colonel Ralph Lane. He was in charge of the 600 soldiers. John White was going again to record the experience in pictures. Wanchese was returning, but Manteo had decided to stay in England another year. Raleigh wanted to go, but Queen Elizabeth insisted he stay at court.

The first trip had gone very well. But this second trip went wrong from the start. The squadron set sail on April 9, 1585. In all, there were seven ships of different sizes. A storm blew up near Portugal. One of the pinnaces sank. The rest of the ships were separated. Eventually the men on the *Tiger* landed in Puerto Rico. They built another pinnace and a temporary fort while waiting for the others. One of the ships finally showed up, but none of the other five ships made it to Puerto Rico.

On June 26, the Englishmen entered an inlet at Wococon off the Outer Banks. A terrible storm called a nor'easter blew up. The *Tiger* was grounded in heavy seas. Much of the food that was to last the men months was ruined. Many thought it was another bad omen.

Grenville decided to explore the surrounding bays and rivers. He wanted to search for a larger and more suitable area for a colony. It was important to find a place where large ships could anchor close to shore. Messages went to Wingina and other weroances about the planned expedition. Grenville and his fifty men, including White and Hariot, rowed across the sound to the village of Pomeioc. They went from there to Aquascogoc. The Native Americans entertained the soldiers. The visitors in turn gave presents to the leaders as tokens of friendship. But after all the feasting, the Europeans discovered that a silver goblet was missing. The explorers continued their mission, but Grenville was furious.

On their way home, Grenville discussed the missing silver goblet with his men. Grenville thought they should get the goblet back, but his men argued with him. They said it was too small an issue to worry about.

But Grenville decided that one of the Native Americans had stolen it and the village must be taught a lesson. If the goblet was returned, he would let the matter pass. If the villagers did not return it or denied they had it, Grenville was ready to take action.

Captain Amadas was ordered by Grenville to find the goblet. Amadas and his soldiers went after it.

Sir Richard Grenville, the man in charge of the first English settlement on Roanoke. He made enemies with the Native Americans, even after they had given him food and help, by attacking and burning one of their villages. This would later have a disastrous effect on the lives of Roanoke settlers.

When the natives did not return it, the soldiers destroyed their corn and burned the village.

The word spread. Though the Native Americans continued to behave in a friendly fashion, a big change had taken place. They grew suspicious of the English. Some of them even grew hostile. The English continued to write glowing reports home. They did not realize the damage that they had done.

White and Hariot were a good balance for the more hot-tempered team of Lane and Grenville. Lane and Grenville didn't get along with each other. They did not work well with the Native Americans either. Part of this was due to their belief that primitive people were their inferiors. The "Indians" were somewhere above a servant, but below an equal. Englishmen also regarded it as their right to intrude on American soil and occupy whatever parts they felt necessary. To simplify, this was a part of their religion. Anyone who wasn't a Christian was a savage. Although the Englishmen's first goal was clearly to establish a colony, their second goal was to spread Christianity.

Hariot and White were interested in the Native American culture. They saw Wingina as curious and receptive. Wingina could have made it very difficult for the settlers if he had wanted. But he was welcoming and generous. His brother and father encouraged friendship with the new people.

At the end of summer, Grenville departed. He left only 106 men behind. The English had arrived too late to plant crops. They were dependent on the Native Americans for food. Wingina and his people were willing to share. But more and more demands from the English for food were beginning to put a strain on their new friendship.

It was a mild winter. Lane decided to explore further north. With fifty men, he ventured up rivers. He stopped in many little villages. When they came to a village called Choanoke, he met an aging, crippled king, Menatonon. Lane took Menatonon as a prisoner for a couple of days and pumped him for information. Menatonon was wise and did not resist. He told Lane about a deep-water bay where there were valuable pearls. Lane and the other settlers were hoping to discover some metal or gems. After all, the Spanish had discovered silver in South America.

At first Lane decided to find this deep-water bay. He told Menatonon he would need guides, food, and a large work crew. Then he changed his mind. He decided to wait for Grenville to return. In the meantime, Lane decided to explore in a different direction.

Around this time, something unusual began to happen. Every time they came upon a village, it was empty. The natives had fled. Did Wingina or others pass the word along? Wingina was upset over the cup incident. And he was upset that Lane kept demanding the corn stored to feed his people.

Lane felt betrayed by the Native Americans. His men were hungry. Lane and his men discussed whether to return to Roanoke. But they decided to keep searching for the copper and pearls that would bring wealth. Suddenly, to their shock, they were attacked by the Native Americans. The soldiers shot at their attackers. Then the soldiers turned and fled.

Lane and his men made it back to Choanoke. This time he took the beloved son of Menatonon, Skikko, as prisoner. Menatonon offered pearls for his release, but Lane said no. Menatonon agreed to acknowledge the queen of England as their only sovereign if Lane would return his son. Lane refused.

Skikko told Lane that Wingina and Wanchese were plotting to kill him and his men. Wingina was already refusing to provide food. Lane ordered his men to collect all the canoes of the Indians. While carrying out Lane's orders, they beheaded two of the natives and shot several others. How had such a peaceful beginning turned into this nightmare?

Lane decided to attack before he was attacked. He and his men went to Wingina's village. Lane told Wingina that one of Wingina's men had stolen his prisoner, Skikko. Wingina told Lane and his men to enter his campsite to discuss it. Some of Wingina's werowances were seated on mats around a fire. "Christ our Victory!" Lane shouted. It was the battle cry of the English. His men opened fire on the natives. Wingina fell to the ground. While the soldiers were attacking others, Wingina ran into the woods. Lane's servant took off after him and returned a few minutes later carrying Wingina's head. Wingina's family had urged him to trust and befriend the English. Wingina had been friendly, but he was betrayed by the greed of the English.

After the battle, which Lane won, he was still worried. Grenville still hadn't appeared. His men were beginning to starve. But it wasn't long before this problem was solved. Sir Francis Drake, another of England's great warriors and explorers, appeared with twenty-seven ships.

The two leaders met. It was decided that Drake would leave ships, supplies, and men for Lane. Grenville had still not shown up.

For the English, one bad event followed another. Just when they felt the "Indian problem" had been settled, a hurricane hit the coast. It practically destroyed Drake's fleet. Drake wanted to set sail immediately. This time Lane decided to leave, with Drake. Drake's men were in a panic to load up and get away from these shores. They threw boxes of White's drawings overboard in the rush.

Lane knew that if everyone left, they would be giving up their claim to this land. They were now on terrible terms with the natives. It is amazing that any of his soldiers chose to stay, but fifteen volunteered to remain until the relief ships came. They must have been offered a large sum of money. The fifteen brave men waved from shore as the ships bearing their friends and countrymen sailed off to England. They would never see each other again.

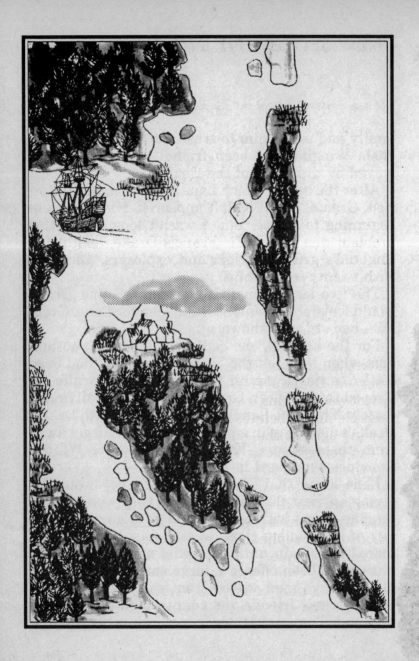

Trouble

John White and Thomas Hariot sat next to each other on Drake's ship heading back to England. Hariot was grieving over the death of his friend Wingina. He didn't believe Lane's story about Wingina plotting against the English.

"I'm going back to Virginia," declared White. "I love the wild country. I believe in the goodness of the native people of America. Perhaps with the right leader, we can live beside them in trust and friendship. My dream is to settle the Chesapeake area."

Hariot had replied, "I wonder about the goodness of our own people."

White was true to his word. A year later, in 1587, he was on a ship headed to Virginia. He was now governor. Though very little is known about his life, from his drawings and his notebooks we know that

White had a deep respect for nature and man. The Native Americans in his drawings are proud and gentle. He learned both their language and their ways. He had a deep respect for what he had seen. Perhaps he would be a better governor than someone like Lane, who never really wanted to know the natives.

White looked at the faces of the other passengers on the ship. His daughter Eleanor was sleeping. White wondered if he was a fool for allowing Eleanor and her husband, Ananias Dare, to come on this voyage. It would be different if she weren't pregnant. But she was a stubborn one, that Eleanor. She had insisted.

It bothered John White that by 1587, many gentlemen involved with Virginia had started to lose interest in the colony. Even Raleigh was shifting his attention to South America. And all the talk in England was of war with the Spanish.

White missed his friend Hariot. But Hariot was busy with a book. White felt that the last months in Virginia had disillusioned Hariot. Amadas and Barlowe, Ralph Lane, Sir Richard Grenville, as well as Hariot were never to return to the Outer Banks.

Fernandes was pilot once again. Captain Edward Stafford was returning, and Edward Spicer was ship's captain. White had accepted Fernandes as an Assistant. But he wasn't pleased about it. The two were so different. Fernandes was in the exploration business for the privateering. All he cared about was the loot. White was an idealist. He wanted to prove that the English could establish a brotherhood in America with the natives.

Who were the people White had talked into selling their belongings and moving to a new world? Moving to Virginia in 1587 would be like volunteering to live on the moon today.

Most of the settlers were from London. They came from the lower-middle class. The offer of 500 acres of uncleared land and the opportunity to become "gentlemen" had strong appeal for them. Each Assistant would receive a coat of arms once he arrived in Virginia. This made him a gentleman. Back in England, citizens showed their social status by their clothing, hairstyles, and special badges they wore. If you dressed above your station, you were punished.

Some settlers may also have gone along as indentured servants. Indentured servents signed an agreement to work for someone for room and board only. They earned their freedom after a certain amount of time. This was a way to pay for one's passage. Although there were some who could pay full fare, others had to work their way over.

Some of the colonists may have wanted more religious freedom. Others may have thought the New World offered a better life. There were fourteen families in all. It seemed cruel to take children on such dangerous trips, but London was filthy. It was filled with disease, and many families no doubt chose Virginia over the unhealthy climate of the city.

White was sad and angry about the massacre that had occurred the year before. But he was convinced that the English could still live alongside the Native Americans. They would be near different tribes in a different location.

Raleigh had given them strict orders on what to do when they arrived in Virginia. They were to check on the fifteen men Lane had left on Roanoke Island. Then they were supposed to head on to the Chesapeake area. White had cannons, handguns, and armor in case they needed to defend themselves.

Manteo was returning on this voyage. Manteo and White had become good friends. Manteo had adopted many English ways, including Christianity. Under Sir Walter Raleigh and the queen, Manteo was to be made lord and ruler of Roanoke Island. It was thought he would be added protection for the colonists once they settled farther upstream.

White's journal is all that is known about the 1587 voyage. According to him, before they were out to sea, Fernandes took command of the expedition. They lost their supply ship almost immediately. White was furious and blamed Fernandes.

The ships were small. Passengers had to remain below deck with little light or air. Cannons were in the portholes. A hatch covering the lower decks was kept on most of the time in case of a storm.

A replica of the ship used by the Roanoke settlers to travel across the Atlantic to their new home.

The voyages were hard on the crew, too. They had to sail around the clock, because there was no way to carry enough line to drop anchor in the middle of the ocean. Unlike the passengers, crew members slept out in the open on the top deck. It must have been miserable sailing. Even the supplies were scanty. Each ship carried enough beer for each man to have one gallon of beer per day. The main rations were a cracker-like bread called hardtack and salt-pork, salted fish, and cheese.

On July 22, the ship carrying White arrived at Port Ferdinando. The colonists went up on deck to have their first look at their new home. The children came up onto the deck first. Their eyes blinked in the bright summer light. In the distance, they could see the land they would call home. There was no sign of human life anywhere.

White went aboard Captain Stafford's pinnace. They sailed through Pamlico Sound to Roanoke Island. A gentleman whom White didn't know came up before they left. "All the plans have changed," he announced.

Simon Fernandes ordered that the planters be left on Roanoke Island. Fernandes would carry them no further! He claimed that it was too late in the season to continue on!

What was White to do? He worried that if he argued with Fernandes, violence might result and some of the colonists might get hurt. But White knew Raleigh's order had been very clear. He was to find the fifteen men left behind, then continue on to Chesapeake Bay. There the colonists would establish the city of Raleigh.

There was nothing the colonists could do but obey the evil Fernandes. White and forty men went to find the fifteen soldiers left behind the year before. The group walked to the homes and fort built the previous year by the soldiers. It was obvious that no one had been there for a long time. Deer were eating melons that were growing out of the dirt floors.

TROUBLE

While White was inside looking for clues, one of his Assistants came running.

Nearby, the men were standing in a circle looking at the bleached bones of a human. Was it one of their soldiers?

White told his men they needed to talk to Manteo to find out what had happened. In the meantime the group decided not to tell the women what they had seen. The men buried the skeleton. It was time to bring the women and children ashore.

On July 25, the missing boat showed up. Everyone rejoiced. White began to feel that coming to Roanoke Island wasn't a mistake after all. He was on familiar ground. It would take time, but they could move to Chesapeake before winter set in.

Although they still hadn't seen any signs of the Native Americans, White would try to establish contact with them over the next few days. For now, he could relax.

The following morning, one of the Assistants, George Howe, came by. He was going crabbing and asked John White to join him. White said no because he wanted to head for Croatoan with Manteo to find Manteo's people as soon as possible.

Howe went crabbing alone. When he didn't return, the settlers went looking for him. Two miles from the campsite they found his body. He had sixteen arrow wounds and his head had been beaten in.

Two days later, Captain Stafford, Manteo, and twenty men went to Croatoan. As the English grew closer, they saw the Croatoans on the beach. The Croatoans were ready to attack until they recognized Manteo. Captain Stafford greeted the Croatoans and told them that this group of English came to renew the old love and to live among them as brothers and friends. Stafford implored their old friends to help them make peace with the other natives. He wanted the natives to forgive and forget. The Croatoans told Stafford that they would bring the chiefs and kings from the different tribes to Governor White within a week.

Stafford asked about the fifteen soldiers. He was told that they had been attacked by Wingina's men from the towns of Secotan, Aquascogoc, and Dasamonquepeuc. One Englishman was killed. The others fought desperately for their lives. They made it to their boat. They had last been seen on a small island near Hatarask. The Croatoans didn't know what happened after that.

What about Howe? The Croatoans reported that he had been killed by some of Wingina's men who kept company with Wanchese. Before Stafford and his men left, the Croatoans asked for a special badge that they could wear. That way the English wouldn't mistake them for the enemy. One of their men lay crippled because he had been mistaken for one of

The new settlers from England at first enjoyed good relations with the Native Americans. They learned a great deal from them about survival. Here is an English depiction of the natives fishing. Note the dug-out canoe, and the abundant and exotic life forms under the water.

Wingina's men the year before. Stafford said that he would talk to White about it.

After White received Stafford's report, he waited for word from the werowances. As the days passed, no word came. His Assistants and other members of the colony became more and more anxious.

Finally, it was agreed that Captain Stafford and twenty-four men, with Manteo acting as guide, would attack the town where Wanchese was. As they approached in the pre-dawn light, they could make out several natives sitting around a fire. Stafford and his men rushed in. They shot one man and were closing in around the others. All of a sudden, one of the natives shouted, "Captain Stafford!" The men halted. They were attacking some of Manteo's people! They had come to collect corn after the Roanokes had fled. What a horrible mistake! Manteo grew angry at his people for not having come to Governor White to talk. That night White was very depressed. No one spoke as they sat around staring into the flames of the bonfire. Everyone wondered why Manteo's people had not come to talk to the English men. The English thought the Indians were their friends. Had Wanchese's people told Manteo's people not to go? No one knew.

Five days later, on August 18, a daughter was born to Eleanor and Ananias Dare. They called her Virginia. She was the first Christian born in Virginia. She was a symbol of hope to the colonists.

The baptism of Manteo, a Native American, in 1587. He later left for England with Sir Richard Grenville and others, and spent two years there before returning. While away, he helped write a dictionary of his language for the settlers to use.

The colonists' first weeks in the new land had not been pleasant or easy. White hoped the birth of his granddaughter marked a change in the colonists' lives in this new world.

The men in the group met. It was decided that one or two of them should return to England with Fernandes and bring back more supplies for the colonists.

At first, a man named Christopher Cooper offered to go. But the next day, Cooper changed his mind. The colonists met again. It looked like a storm was building at sea. Fernandes wouldn't wait much longer.

The group decided John White should return with Fernandes. He was reluctant. He felt he had too much to do. It was his job to lead the colonists to a safer place. He had sworn to Raleigh and to the queen he would establish a colony in Virginia before the Spanish did.

White was also afraid that people in England would feel he abandoned the colonists. Most of all he was reluctant to leave his family behind. He asked Eleanor and her husband Ananias Dare what they felt he should do.

Eleanor did not want her father to leave, but she felt someone had to return to England. The group had decided that person was White, and the majority must rule.

The colonists put in writing that they had chosen White to go. The colonists agreed to take good care of his trunks of drawings and papers. They would expect him back within six months. Ninety-one men, seventeen women, nine children, and two babies born in Virginia would be waiting for his return. It was a total of 119 people.

TROUBLE

White packed up the settlers' letters home. He climbed aboard the pinnace that would take him out to where Fernandes was anchored. His friends and family waved until he was out of sight.

Words

"Eleanor!" White yelled as he ran into the clearing on Roanoke Island. He stopped to get his breath. He looked around.

The men searched frantically for signs. Before White left for England it was agreed that if the colonists had to leave Roanoke, they would carve a message in one of the trees or on a post near the houses.

Then he saw it. Some letters were carved on a tree up ahead. He struggled through the sand to the tree. Carved there were the letters CRO. White put his hand up and traced the letters with his finger.

The group felt it must mean Croatoan. The colonists were probably at Croatoan with Manteo!

But the word *Croatoan* was not spelled out. Did it really mean Croatoan? Were the colonists in too big a hurry to carve the whole word? White remembered that they had agreed to carve the symbol of the Mal-

John White finally returns to Roanoke and discovers the mysterious message "Croatoan" carved into a tree. The man kneeling to the right is opening a chest that they found buried in the sand containing important papers.

tese cross if the group had to leave in distress. But if they really had had to leave in distress, would they have had time to carve the cross?

White and his men searched further. The houses had been torn down. Where the houses had been was a palisade of great trees. It looked like a fort. To the right of the entrance the bark had been taken off a post. The word CROATOAN was carved into the post. Again, there was no sign of a cross.

The men entered the fort. They found bars of iron, lead, a light cannon, and other such things. Grass and weeds had grown over them.

White went to see if any boats had been left. One

of Cocke's men came running up while White was walking along the water's edge. They had found five trunks.

When White and Cocke arrived on the scene, White discovered many of his personal things lying about. The books had been torn from their covers, and his maps were rotten from the rain and dampness. His armor was eaten through with rust.

The men were becoming more convinced that the settlers really did have to leave in a hurry. The English believed it was the Indians who had done all the damage. They thought Wingina's people may have waited until the colonists left, and then returned to destroy everything.

The men continued to search for clues. One minute, White was sure that the colonists would be in Croatoan. The next minute, he would have doubts. Their plan had been to go to the Chesapeake Bay area. On the other hand, maybe they had gone to Croatoan to be under Manteo's protection. There they could keep watch for the sight of English ships.

White suggested to Cocke that they continue their search for the colonists on Croatoan the next day. White was sure the colonists would be there. He and Cocke planned to sail there, find the colonists, and then return for the barrels of fresh water.

The men agreed to the plan. But it looked as if a storm was coming in. Both Cocke and White were worried. They knew now how weather could suddenly change in the Outer Banks. Sir Francis Drake said that nothing had damaged his ships as much as the storm he went through in the Outer Banks.

The following morning, Cocke and White got ready to sail for Croatoan. Sea conditions were rough. Just as they were prepared to leave, an anchor cable broke. The ship lost her anchor. They were driven toward land and almost crashed against rocks. They were stuck. Now their ship had one anchor and one cable. There were usually four. The men were nearly out of fresh water, too.

Cocke talked White into going for fresh water. At first they thought they would sail to the Caribbean and return in a few days. Again, the weather didn't cooperate. They decided to go to another group of islands. This time, weather prevented them from approaching land.

Privateering was more popular than ever. Cocke, like most English captains of that era, loved to find prizes. He was hoping to join a great fleet of English ships that was searching for a Spanish treasure fleet. The English fleet was rumored to be near the coast of America, but Cocke's group missed it. Cocke and his crew were still without water. Winds had not allowed them to go ashore.

"I think we should head back to England," Cocke announced to White. "It's mid-September and the weather will only get worse." He continued, "I've lost two boats on this voyage. Our ship is missing an anchor and a cable. We still don't have water."

White listened as the captain went on with his

reasons. He replied, "I'm afraid that if we leave, I will never get back. I have spent the past three years trying to return to Virginia. What if Sanderson won't come up with the money for another voyage?"

Cocke was sympathetic, but firm. "We really don't have a choice. It's too dangerous. The weather has not improved in weeks."

"Then I can do nothing but agree," White replied.

White was saddened by his luck. "These people went in the name of England to build a country!" he said. "They are the founders of the New World! Doesn't anybody care? How can we leave them? Wanchese and his people may have killed them. Or the Spanish could have killed them! It is dangerous to be in Virginia with no supplies and so few people!"

White wrote in his journal, "They will all be forgotten. Those brave, good people will all be forgotten."

White thought back to his departure from Virginia three years earlier. He had told the colonists he would be back in Virginia within six to eight months.

He thought back over the past six years. There had been many serious mistakes. Why did Grenville burn a village because of a stolen cup? Why didn't Lane realize that murdering the chief Wingina would start a war? Why did Lane and Drake leave only fifteen men on the island when they returned to England? Why did the relief ship return to England rather than wait for Grenville's fleet?

And Fernandes! If only they had continued on to

The town of Secotan, from another drawing by John White.
Secotan was a larger and more populous town than
Pomeiooc. It was better protected and needed no
surrounding barrier.

the Chesapeake Bay instead of being dropped by Fernandes in an unknown place. He might be sitting with his family now. Raleigh had been angry with Fernandes when they returned to England, but Fernandes knew his knowledge and skill would save him. White wanted Fernandes jailed, but nothing would ever happen.

White was angry at the government-endorsed privateering that had interfered with his search. If the ships hadn't been so long in the Caribbean on this voyage, would things have been different? Had spending the one day following the distant smoke instead of going straight to Roanoke Island made a difference?

White would try to return again. As soon as the ships were back in England, he would implore Raleigh and Sanderson to organize another trip to Virginia. The next time, White would make sure they went straight to Croatoan.

And if the settlers weren't at Croatoan, at least they would find Manteo. He could tell them where they had gone. Did they move north to live with the Chesapeake Indians? Or into the interior to join Menatonon's Chawanoacs? Were they in one of the villages such as Pomeiooc or Secotan? Another question was haunting White. It was a question he tried not to ask. Did Wanchese take revenge against the English? A shudder went up White's spine as he remembered the fate of the fifteen soldiers.

He would never stop searching. He knew that.

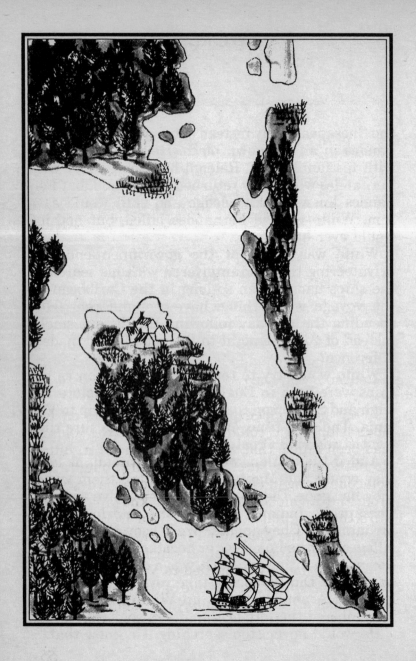

The Theories

The same thoughts and questions John White asked 400 years ago are in many people's minds today.

What had happened to the first settlers on Roanoke Island? If it could be proven that the colonists had been killed, that would be the end of it. But we do not know for sure. There is still a chance that someone living in North Carolina today is descended from the Roanoke colonists. Not knowing for sure stirs the imagination. Did Virginia Dare grow up? Eleanor and her daughter Virginia still stand at the beginning of North Carolina's history.

What ultimately happened to Virginia's grandfather, John White? He was one of the main players in the drama of the early colony. He did attempt one more trip across the Atlantic Ocean, but it, too, failed. After that, he disappears from English history, just as his family disappeared from the shores of the Outer Banks. He tried to find the money to go back, but his energy wasn't the same. In 1593, three years after his return to England, he wrote that the relief of the colony was left to the merciful help of the Almighty. He added in his letter, "I would to God my wealth were answerable to my will." Sir Walter Raleigh had the wealth, but his interests had shifted to other countries. Raleigh backed another privateering fleet in 1591. But they went nowhere near the Outer Banks. Finally, in 1602, Raleigh decided to search again for the colonists. It had been fifteen years. His patent was about to run out. He needed to prove that the settlers were still on Virginia land. But the ships he sent ran into the same problem: bad weather. They turned around and came home to England, never stopping in Virginia.

Today, most of what we know about Roanoke Island comes from journals and papers written by the adventurers. We have also learned things from studying old maps, including some drawn by John White. Archeological diggings might uncover more clues. The full story will probably never be known.

Spanish records were studied long after the disappearance of the colonists. These records report that when Amadas and Barlowe went to Chesapeake Bay in 1584, a few of their men were killed by members of the Powhatan tribe. Did the later colonists meet with the same fate?

White and his Assistants had talked about dividing the colonists into two groups. A small group would await White's arrival on Roanoke Island. The larger group would continue to Chesapeake Bay. It is obvious that when White returned in 1590, he wasn't clear about what they had decided to do. When White saw CROATOAN carved on the post, he was thrilled. He was hoping that all of them had gone to Manteo's island. But a lot of that could have been his wishful thinking.

Over the years, many people have come up with theories about the fate of the colonists. The most common theory is that the colonists intermixed with the Native Americans. But which tribe did they join?

In 1660, a minister said that he preached in the Neuse River area to Indians who were light-colored and who spoke Welsh. Years later, the explorer John Lederer visited an area where a group of bearded men were seated. He thought they were probably of Spanish descent, as it was believed Native Americans did not have beards. Historians today question these accounts. For example, according to Hariot's writings, the Native Americans in Pomeioc were growing beards.

In the 1700s, a man named John Lawson wrote a book about North Carolina. He included the Lost

Colony in it. He writes about the Hatteras Indians, who told him that their ancestors were white people and "could talk in a Book." The writer went on to say that he noticed gray eyes among some of those Indians. Historians think they could be descended from Raleigh's colonists, but which ones? There were fifteen men left there before Lane's soldiers showed up.

There is also a North Carolina legend that comes from Native American folklore. The story claims that the ship which brought the first colonists appears from time to time under full sail. They call it Sir Walter Raleigh's ship.

Very little was written about the Lost Colony for 250 years. Then, in the mid-nineteenth century, a North Carolina historian wrote that he thought the settlers had starved to death. The historian believed that all the islands in the Outer Banks were low, bare, and had no wild food or game. The truth is that many of them are fertile and contain edible plants and wildlife. Although it is possible the colonists starved to death, it is also possible that they could have survived.

In 1890, a man named Hamilton McMillan developed a theory. Near him was a settlement of "persons of mixed color." In that area they were called Indians. They were not accepted at the white schools and they refused to attend the black schools. They were very poor. They clung to their Indian traditions. They believed that they were descended from a mixture of Native Americans and the early English settlers. They claimed their birthplace was Roanoke, in Virginia.

McMillan said their language was almost pure Anglo-Saxon. Many of their words were no longer used in modern times. McMillan next studied the writings of a famous English historian named Hakluyt, who wrote during the 1580s. Hakluyt mentions many family names that are the same as those listed among the lost colonists. The tribe in Robeson County was "a proud race, boasting alike of their English and Indian blood." McMillan was sure that he had solved the mystery of the lost colony.

In 1885, North Carolina passed an act that ordered that separate schools were to be provided for the Croatoan Indians in Robeson County. Another North Carolina historian wrote in 1891 that of the ninety-five different surnames listed among the colonists, forty-one were the same as those of the tribe living in Robeson County and listed on the school roster. Robeson County is hundreds of miles from Roanoke Island.

When the Native Americans wanted their tribe to be recognized, someone from the United States Bureau of Indian Affairs went to check out their identity. He said that the Indians in Robeson County were the descendants of the Hatteras Indians and Governor White's colony.

This information seemed to provide the answer so

many were searching for. But many didn't accept it. McMillan thought the Hatteras Indians had migrated over 200 miles west to the Lumber River, where he discovered them.

A later historian was convinced that the colonists had moved west to the banks of the Chowan River. Another declared that the colonists had been attacked at the fort on Roanoke Island by followers of Wanchese and Powhatan. Those colonists who escaped went in different directions.

In London's *Cornhill* magazine, a writer concluded that the colonists were attacked by the Spaniards. That was a very real worry for the English during those years. It is known that the Spaniards organized an expedition to the area in 1588. But it is also known that as late as 1600, the Spaniards were still looking for the colony in the Outer Banks. They thought all along that the colonists were on the Chesapeake Bay.

One modern researcher named Don Austin believes that descendants of the forgotten colony still live in the villages of the Outer Banks, the islands of the H'atarask tribe. He says, "A lot of the older people there who remember their grandparents and great-grandparents will tell you how dark they were. We even called my grandmother 'Blackma!'"

In 1937, Paul Green wrote his famous outdoor drama, *The Lost Colony*. Franklin Roosevelt, President of the United States at that time, went to see it.

THE THEORIES

It is still presented on Roanoke Island near Fort Raleigh every year during the summer. Thousands have watched the mastheads of the ships moving eerily along the back of the stage fort, bringing the make-believe colonists to Roanoke Island. The fact that the drama is presented outdoors makes all the characters seem larger than life. At the end of the play, Green has the planters and Assistants heading to Croatoan.

Another story came to light that had people's imaginations churning. In 1938, the vice president of a college in Georgia announced that a man had brought him a twenty-one-pound stone. The stone was found on the bank of the Chowan River. There was writing on it signed with the initials of Eleanor White Dare—E.W.D. Another stone was found later in a part of Georgia. This continued. Forty-nine stones turned up! The press began to refer to them as Eleanor Dare's diary. The college official took them to stonecutters and other experts. He was told that they had to be very old. He took them to geologists. They agreed with the stonecutters. He took them to Elizabethan English experts. They said the words and writing were accurate. Finally, a panel of historians went to the college. They believed the stones were real.

A reporter from a national magazine went down to write a story. He checked with the stonecutters, the geologists, and the experts on Elizabethan English.

The Dare Stone, which was one of forty-nine stones found in a great hoax in 1938, can now be seen in the museum at Brenau College in Gainesville, Georgia.

THE THEORIES

They had not been quoted correctly. All had found flaws in the stones. The "diary" was finally traced to a Roanoke Island man who created the hoax with the hope of selling the stones for a lot of money.

The hoax didn't stop the search for the lost colony. In 1946, two men published a book stating that Roanoke Island was not the home of the colony at all. In 1954, two North Carolina historians suggested that the group, giving up on relief, sailed for England in a boat White had left behind. They were lost in the Atlantic.

What makes the most sense today are the reports of the Jamestown settlers. They were the only people who tried to make contact with any living lost colonists. They believed that the Roanoke settlers probably moved in the fall of 1587. They would want to be in their new homes before winter set in. Much then depended on the Chesapeake Indians at Skicoak. It is likely that the colonists would have set up their homes near the Indian village. The land was richer than the land on the coast. The settlers could grow their own gardens.

From 1587 to 1603, nothing is known about the colonists. But once they accepted that John White wasn't coming back, they probably moved into deeper relationships with the Native Americans.

This brings the story to Powhatan, a powerful chief who had taken over a number of tribes along the Chesapeake. He did not succeed with the Chesapeakes, the tribe the English had come upon years before. Powhatan, unlike the kings on Roanoke Island and nearby places, did not like the idea of anyone entering his territory. His priests had foretold the arrival of a white man, come to take away his kingdom. It is believed that Powhatan knew about the white people living with his neighbors on the Chesapeake. For twenty years they had lived in peace. But when Powhatan got wind of more white men coming to settle on the Chesapeake, he massacred the members of White's colony.

The members of John Smith's colony knew about the lost colony. They had been instructed by some of their supporters in London to look for the missing colonists. One man from John Smith's Jamestown colony wrote about a trip he made into the heart of Virginia in 1607. They saw "a savage Boy about the age of ten years, which had a head of hair of a perfect yellow and a reasonable white skin, which is a miracle amongst all Savages." Later, Captain John Smith wrote about the lost colonists in a book. He reported that he had met a certain Indian king who had told him about men who were clothed just like Smith. Another chief spoke of a place called Anone where the people had a lot of brass and houses that were built like the English houses in Jamestown. Yet another group of governors wrote that their men reported finding crosses and letters newly cut into the bark of trees.

THE THEORIES

Captain John Smith was also a mapmaker. In a chart that he sent back to England he marked a spot and wrote that "here remain four men clothed that came from Roanoke to Ocanahawan."

In 1609, members of the Virginia Company wrote to England about four Englishmen who had escaped the slaughter of Powhatan. They said that the four lived under the protection of a werowance. This was never proved, and these four men were never found.

In 1612, another Englishman wrote about a village not far from Jamestown that had English-style houses. He said that the Indians were taught by the English who had escaped Powhatan. He claimed that there were seven English alive—four men, two boys, and one young maid. Was the young maid Virginia Dare?

What Really Happened?

The actions of the 119 men, women, and children left on Roanoke Island is a mystery that has teased writers and historians for over 400 years. Why should it concern anyone whether the colonists went to Chesapeake or drowned at sea? Does it matter if they survived or not? It does matter, because they are our spiritual ancestors. They were real people trying to exist in an unexplored land. Their names are listed in the journals of John White. Much of who we are today comes from our forefathers. If they hadn't been so courageous, the Spanish might have colonized Virginia first, and the whole history of our country would be different. Today some historians feel that North Carolina—not New England—is really the birthplace of our country.

It is almost certain that some of the colonists went

on and lived among the Chesapeakes. The stories are too consistent and too plentiful not to have some truth in them. It was unusual for Native Americans to kill women and children. If some did escape Powhatan's attack, which many historians believe occurred, then they may have descendents in North Carolina today. Was Virginia Dare the maiden the Jamestown colonists heard about? If some went to Croatoan to wait for relief, did they stay or did they make their way to the Chesapeake later on? If they did head north, why didn't they go back to Roanoke Island and change the carving on the tree? Did they ever stop hoping that their English brothers would come? Indians told stories of white men working in copper mines near Jamestown. Were these stories true and did these men know about the Roanoke colonists? Were the colonists prisoners of the Native Americans?

What is most curious is that the Roanoke Island settlers seem to have disappeared from the history books, too. One native of North Carolina believes that this is because the settlers at Roanoke were not upper-class like those who landed at Plymouth. Whatever the reason, the colonists today live mainly in the imagination of historians and archeologists who carry on a never-ending search for more information.

It is a tragic story, a story without a happy ending. Some of it is about failure. The failure is not that the colonists disappeared. The ones who failed were not the planters and Assistants who helped carve the way for others. The failure lies with people like Lane and Grenville who were arrogant and filled with racial pride. These men needed to control others. They did not make it easy for the families who came later. They destroyed the idea of one brotherhood.

The others who failed were the high officials in England. They abandoned the people they had sent to establish a colony on an island. They knew that the colonists were stranded. John White pleaded over and over for their cause. He surely told the high officials how dangerous conditions were on Roanoke Island. They sacrificed the 119 colonists for greed and the sake of war.

Is there a leftover sense of guilt? Is there something that makes people cringe at the thought of leaving the settlers to wander lost through the woods? Is there a feeling of shame deep down inside over the way the English soldiers behaved towards fellow human beings? Long before the English moved into the New World, it was acceptable to overcome native peoples with violence and to take their land. The Spanish exploration of Mexico and the American Southwest is a good example of that.

When Barlowe and Amadas arrived in Virginia, they found people who were vastly different from Europeans. The inhabitants had been called Indians by the white man since the time Columbus discovered America. That is the name they gave to people they considered savages in other countries. It didn't matter that these natives had a group name and identity. What surprised the English was that the Native Americans had an organized society that worked very well. The English had already entered the Iron Age. They were building large cities and opening factories. The people in the New World reminded them of the days when life was simpler and thus, they were considered savages.

There were several reasons why the English were able to gain control so fast. They believed they had a divine right to be there. One of the quests of the Europeans was to spread the word of their religion and convert the natives in whatever way possible.

The weapons of the English gave them tremendous power. The Native Americans had never seen guns and were terrified of them. They saw the destructiveness of guns and cannons and gave in to the English rather than be killed. But, the silent weapon that most terrified the Natives was sickness. Native Americans felt that often the English would leave illness behind if they were displeased. It wasn't intentional of course. But the natives began to believe that the English were magical and could spread an evil sickness if the natives did not obey. Native Americans had no natural immunity to many of the diseases the English sailors carried with them from England. These diseases could sweep through an In-

A marker commemorating the disappearance at Roanoke Island, and the birth of the first English person born in the New World, a girl named Virginia Dare. It was placed there in 1896.

dian village killing nearly everyone. It was no wonder the Indians feared the whites.

Historians remind their readers to stick to facts. But there is a layer underneath the lost colonists that has nothing to do with facts. It is a story that has been told and retold many times. Plays, stories, books, and articles have been written about it. It is impossible to go to Roanoke Island today and not try to imagine the fate of the colonists. You can stand on the famous sand dunes in Nags Head and imagine a pinnace coming into sight. You can go to the little island of Ocracoke by ferry and imagine the settlers coming up on this island. The long stretches of dunes and beaches between Cape Hatteras and Ocracoke appear today as a vast wilderness. In one direction is the town of Manteo. In another is the village of Wanchese. It is fun to imagine the pinnaces coming ashore at Cape Hatteras or the big ships anchored out at sea.

The Roanoke Sound is the backdrop for the play *The Lost Colony*. As the lights go down, you can be like the people on Cape Hatteras who claim they see the ship, sails unfurled, that belonged to Sir Walter Raleigh. The capital of North Carolina is called Raleigh, another lasting legacy for these lost colonists.

What was it like for the men, women, and children when they began to think no one was coming back with supplies and other family members? John Borden, the hero of the play *The Lost Colony,* speaks

WHAT REALLY HAPPENED?

for the colonists as they prepare to leave Roanoke Island. ". . . down the centuries that wait ahead, there'll be some whisper of our name, some mention and devotion to the dream that brought us here."

John White need not have worried that his family and friends would be forgotten. The mystery of their fate will keep them famous forever.

Bibliography

Arner, Robert D., *The Lost Colony in Literature;* America's Four Hundredth Anniversary Committee, North Carolina Department of Cultural Resources; 1985.

Cumming, William P., *Mapping the North Carolina Coast, Sixteenth-Century Cartography and the Roanoke Voyages;* Division of Archives and History, North Carolina Department of Cultural Resources; 1988.

Harrington, J.C., *Archaeology and the Enigma of Fort Raleigh;* America's Four Hundredth Anniversary Committee; North Carolina Department of Cultural Resources; 1984.

Kupperman, Karen Ordahl, *Roanoke, The Abandoned Colony;* Rowman & Allanheld Publishers, Totowa, New Jersey, 1984.

Porter III, Charles W., *Fort Raleigh and the First English Settlement in the New World;* Division of Publications, National Park Service, U.S. Department of the Interior, Washington, D.C., 1985.

Quinn, David B. Quinn and Alison M., editors, *The First Colonists, Documents on the Planting of the First English Settlements in North America, 1584–1590.*

Quinn, David Beers, *Set Fair for Roanoke: Voyages and Colonies,* 1584–1606; University of North Carolina Press, Chapel Hill, London, 1985.

Stick, David, *Roanoke Island, the Beginnings of English America;* University of North Carolina Press, Chapel Hill and London, 1983.

Periodicals:

Currie, Jack, "Did Lost Silver Cup Lead to Lost Colony?"; The Daily Advance; September 4, 1983.

Green, Paul, "A Backward Look With a Forward Hope," The News And Observer, Raleigh, N.C.; July 1, 1962.

BIBLIOGRAPHY

Landau, Debora, "Fate of Lost Colony Gives Rise to Different Theories," Outer Banks Current; February 23, 1989.

Photo Credits

Interior photographs are credited as follows:

Page viii: Courtesy of the Roanoke Island Historical Association.

Page 5: Courtesy of the North Carolina State Department of Cultural Resources, Division of Archives and History.

Page 10: From *Roanoke Island, The Beginnings of English America* by David Stick, © 1983, University of North Carolina Press. Reprinted by permission of the publisher.

Page 16: From *America 1585: The Complete Drawings of John White* by Paul Huston, © 1984, University of North Carolina Press. Drawings © 1964, The Trustees of the British Museum. Used with permission of the publisher.

Page 19: From *Roanoke Island, The Beginnings of English America* by David Stick, © 1983, University of North Carolina Press. Reprinted by permission of the publisher.

Page 21: Courtesy of the North Carolina State Department of Cultural Resources, Division of Archives and History.

Page 23: Courtesy of the North Carolina State Department of Cultural Resources, Division of Archives and History.

Page 27: Courtesy of the North Carolina State Department of Cultural Resources, Division of Archives and History.

Page 37: Courtesy of The Elizabeth II, State Historic Site, Manteo, North Carolina, and the North Carolina Department of Cultural Resources. Photograph by Joe Ernst.

Page 41: Courtesy of the North Carolina State Department of Cultural Resources, Division of Archives and History.

Page 43: Courtesy of the North Carolina Collection, University of North Carolina Library at Chapel Hill.

Page 48: Courtesy of the North Carolina State Department of Cultural Resources, Division of Archives and History.

Page 52: From *America 1585: The Complete Drawings of John White* by Paul Huston, © 1984, University of North Carolina Press. Drawings © 1964, The Trustees of the British Museum. Used with permission of the publisher.

Page 62: Courtesy of Brenau College, Gainesville, Georgia.

Page 71: Courtesy of the North Carolina State Department of Cultural Resources, Division of Archives and History.

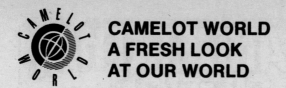

CAMELOT WORLD
A FRESH LOOK
AT OUR WORLD

THE MYSTERIOUS CAT
by Elizabeth Garrick

76038-X/$2.95 US/$3.50 Can

HOT MACHINES
by Gregory Pope

76039-8/$2.95 US/$3.50 Can

SECRETS OF THE SAMURAI
by Carol Gaskin

76040-1/$2.95 US/$3.50 Can

A KID'S GUIDE TO HOW TO SAVE THE PLANET

76041-X/$2.95 US/$3.50 Can

by Billy Goodman

GREAT DISASTERS
by David Keller

76043-6/$2.95 US/$3.50 Can

DOLLS
by Vivian Werner

76044-4/$2.95 US/$3.50 Can

UFOS AND ALIENS
by William R. Alschuler

76045-2/$2.95 US/$3.50 Can

STRANGER THAN FICTION

by MELVIN BERGER

ASTOUND YOUR FRIENDS
WITH INCREDIBLE, LITTLE-KNOWN FACTS ABOUT...

KILLER BUGS   76036-3/$2.95 US/$3.50 Can

More people are killed by insects than by all other animals combined—including sharks and snakes.

DINOSAURS   76052-5/$2.95 US/$3.50 Can

Dinosaurs are the largest, most magnificent and most terrifying creatures that ever roamed the Earth.

MONSTERS   76053-3/$2.95 US/$3.50 Can

Do creatures like Big Foot and the Abominable Snowman really exist?

SEA MONSTERS   76054-1/$2.95 US/$3.50 Can

Unlike the shark in *Jaws*, this book is about the real living sea monsters that swim the waters of the world.